W9-CSK-353

A Birthday Is Beautiful

A Birthday Is Beautiful

Selected by Ruth E. Mohring

Illustrated by Frances Stevens

♛ HALLMARK EDITIONS

A Birthday Is Beautiful

Capricorn-The Goat

December 22 — January 19

Capricornians, with their reserve,
  Seem hard to get to know,
But given time, their sense of humor
  Really steals the show.
They're practical and careful
  And full of common sense,
And because they're conscientious,
  They inspire great confidence.
They're faithful and devoted
  To those they're fondest of,
And they'll do anything on earth
  To help the ones they love.

Things to do on your birthday
under the Sign of Capricorn:

Call an old friend.
Make a new friend.
Have a picnic in the snow.

January

Flower - *Carnation*   Birthstone - *Garnet*

JANUARY 1

Our twelve months go round and round,
The same months every year.
And January starts them off,
The first day icy-clear.

Begin this year as though you too
Were really not the same —
Like every January first,
Brand-new in your old name.

MARNIE POMEROY

All sorts of things and weather
Must be taken in together,
To make up a year
And a sphere.

RALPH WALDO EMERSON

A BIRTHDAY IS BEAUTIFUL

A birthday's a beautiful happening—
The years do not matter
  when the heart is at spring;
Days should be measured
  by the happiness they hold,
For that is a treasure
  much greater than gold.
When the heart is at spring,
  then the mind's always young,
With a promise to seek,
  with a song to be sung.
Yes, a birthday's a beautiful happening,
For age cannot conquer
  the heart that's at spring.

BENJAMIN WHITLEY

THE NEW YEAR

A Flower unblown: a Book unread:
A Tree with fruit unharvested:
A Path untrod: a House whose rooms
Lack yet the heart's divine perfumes:
This is the Year that for you waits
Beyond Tomorrow's mystic gates.

HORATIO NELSON POWERS

At eighteen, one adores at once;
at twenty, one loves;
at thirty, one desires;
at forty, one reflects.

PAUL DE KOCK

8

Aquarius-The Water-Bearer

January 20—February 18

People born under Aquarius
   Are gentle, kind, and giving.
They thrive on change and adventure
   And have great zest for living.
They see a lot of little things
   Most people overlook
And learn as much from experience
   As they do from reading books.
They take whatever life may bring
   And never give in to sorrow,
For they know that something wonderful
   Is sure to come tomorrow.

Things to do on your birthday
under the Sign of Aquarius:

Copy frost patterns off the windows.
Reread *Tom Sawyer.*
Buy a single rose for the table.

February

Flower - *Violet*   Birthstone - *Amethyst*

FEBRUARY TWILIGHT

The woods are blue with shrouding mist,
The lights stand out upon the hill;
A spirit I cannot resist
Calms my own beyond my will.

Upon the ground the snow lies wet,
The water streams, a velvet ooze;
A beech-tree spreads a silver net
To catch the dream I would not lose.

Here in the stillness of this hour,
Deep in the twilight loitering,
Time breathes more lightly than a flower,
Waiting the miracle of spring.

SALLY BRUCE KINSOLVING

OLD ENGLISH PRAYER

Take time to work—
   It is the price of success.
Take time to think—
   It is the source of power.
Take time to play—
   It is the secret of perpetual youth.
Take time to read—
   It is the fountain of wisdom.
Take time to be friendly—
   It is the road to happiness.
Take time to dream—
   It is hitching your wagon to a star.
Take time to love and to be loved—
   It is the privilege of the gods.
Take time to look around—
   It is too short a day to be selfish.
Take time to laugh—
   It is the music of the soul.

A VALENTINE

Do you love me
Or do you not?
You told me once
But I forgot.

COMMONPLACE

"A commonplace life,"
    we say, and we sigh,
But why should we sigh as we say?
The commonplace sun
    in the commonplace sky
Makes up the commonplace day;
The moon and the stars
    are commonplace things,
And the flower that blooms,
    and the bird that sings,
But dark were the world,
    and sad our lot,
If the flowers failed,
    and the sun shone not;
And God, who studies
    each separate soul,
Out of commonplace lives
    makes His beautiful whole.

SUSAN COOLIDGE

No sky at all;
    no earth at all—and still
    the snowflakes fall....

Translated by HAROLD G. HENDERSON

12

Pisces-The Fishes

February 19—March 20

Pisceans are perceptive,
    They have great intuition,
And though they're sometimes timid,
    They work with real ambition.
They're thoughtful, for they understand
    The fears and feelings of others.
They see the world as a beautiful place
    And all men as their brothers.
They're seldom lonely, even when alone;
    They like to draw apart
And think sometimes about the secrets
    Treasured in their hearts.

Things to do on your birthday under the Sign of Pisces:

Buy (and use) a ouija board.
Scatter bread crumbs for the birds.
Listen to Rachmaninoff.

14

March

Flower - *Jonquil*   Birthstone - *Aquamarine*

MARCH DAY

Weather is beguiling—
Not a cloud in sight—
Sun is busy smiling
Down with all his might.

Comes a wind that screeches,
Scattering leaves and trash—
Wailing through the beeches—
Dying in a flash.

Then a sudden flurry—
Pelting flakes of snow
Dancing as they scurry...
Putting on a show.

Every kind of weather
Strutting on display—
All mixed up together...
What a dappled day!

MARY BOYD WAGNER

15

TWELVE DAISIES

How many daisies can you count on your lawn?
    When you can count twelve daisies,
        Spring has come.

SPRING AT THE DOOR

Spring is a wild thing for sure—
    What wilder ever ran?
But once in a while he will rub at the door
    Of almost any man,
And here he is at my own sill,
    Whining for me to know,
Until I peer outside and feel
    A flurry in the snow,
Find a cloud of shining flakes,
    A blur of footprints four,
From a wild thing that comes and shakes
    The quiet of my door.

WITTER BYNNER

WEARING OF THE GREEN

It ought to come in April,
or, better yet, in May
when everything is green as green—
I mean St. Patrick's Day.

With still a week of winter
this wearing of the green
seems rather out of season—
it's rushing things, I mean.

But maybe March IS better
when all is done and said:
St. Patrick brings a promise,
a four-leaf-clover promise,
a green-all-over promise
of springtime just ahead!

AILEEN FISHER

17

Aries—The Ram

March 21—April 20

Arians add a bright touch
To everything,
For theirs is the Sign
Of youth and of spring.
They have a quick temper.
There's little they fear.
They rise to the challenge
When problems appear.
They have high ideals
That set them apart.
They can reach any goal
And win any heart.

Things to do on your birthday
under the Sign of Aries:

Think of something nice you can
do for a friend—and do it.
Call some member of your family
long distance.
Read a best seller.

April

Flower - *Sweet Pea*   Birthstone - *Diamond*

SONG

April, April,
Laugh thy girlish laughter;
Then, the moment after,
Weep thy girlish tears!
April, that mine ears
Like a lover greetest,
If I tell thee, sweetest,
All my hopes and fears,
April, April,
Laugh thy golden laughter,
But the moment after,
Weep thy golden tears!

WILLIAM WATSON

April 1 is the day upon which we are
reminded of what we are on the other 364.

MARK TWAIN

SHEEP AND LAMBS

All in the April morning,
  April airs were abroad;
The sheep with their little lambs
  Pass'd me by on the road.

The sheep with their little lambs
  Pass'd me by on the road;
All in an April evening
  I thought on the Lamb of God.

The lambs were weary, and crying
  With a weak human cry;
I thought on the Lamb of God
  Going meekly to die.

Up in the blue, blue mountains
  Dewy pastures are sweet:
Rest for the little bodies,
  Rest for the little feet.

All in the April evening,
  April airs were abroad;
I saw the sheep with their lambs,
  And thought on the Lamb of God.

KATHARINE TYNAN HINKSON

PASSOVER AND FREEDOM

Passover is the Festival of Spring.
Its human appeal, therefore,
is as old as humanity,
and as perennial as spring.
But it is an historical festival—
Israel's birthday—as the annual
commemoration of an event
which has changed
the destinies of mankind, that proclaims
the man-redeeming truth,
God is the God of Freedom.

MORRIS JOSEPH

OPEN THE DOOR

Open the door, let in the air;
The winds are sweet and the flowers are fair.
Joy is abroad in the world today:
If our door is wide it may come this way—
  Open the door!

Taurus-The Bull

April 21—May 20

Those born under the Taurus Sign
    Count friends more precious than money.
They're faithful to their loved ones
    And their dispositions are sunny.
They tend to feel things more deeply
    Than many people do,
Which brings them anxious moments,
    But radiant happiness, too.
They seem to grow younger every year,
    For their Sign holds the spirit of youth.
They always find joy wherever they look
    In their search for beauty and truth.

Things to do on your birthday
under the Sign of Taurus:

Plant a tree.
Stay in bed all morning.
Buy yourself something frivolous.

May

Flower - *Lily of the Valley* Birthstone - *Emerald*

MAYTIME

The air is filled with fragrance; orchard trees
Like fair young maidens in their pastel gowns
Whisper their secrets and the murmuring sounds
Are caught by vagrant winds that love to tease,
Repeating tales of romance as they seize
And pass this confidence soon lost to bounds;
The brooks join merrily; what joy surrounds
The earth in glad awakening with these.

Nature is kind in Maytime, then is borne
To jaded hearts a newness and desire;
Old dreams revive to make each glowing morn
Alive with eagerness that does not tire;
In glad response to feel the magic sway
Of beauty's charm; this is the gift of May.

DELLA ADAMS LEITNER

Wish not so much to live long, as to live well.

BENJAMIN FRANKLIN

SPRING

Now every field is clothed with grass,
and every tree with leaves;
now the woods put forth their blossoms,
and the year assumes its gay attire.

VIRGIL

Let me but live from year to year,
  With forward face and unreluctant soul;
  Not hurrying to, nor turning from, the goal;
Not mourning for the things that disappear
In the dim past, nor holding back in fear
  From what the future veils, but with a whole
  And happy heart, that pays its toll
To Youth and Age, and travels on with cheer.

HENRY VAN DYKE

ZEST FOR LIFE

I have never been bored an hour in my life.
I get up every morning wondering what new,
strange, glamorous thing is going to happen
and it happens at fairly regular intervals.
Lady Luck has been good to me
and I fancy she has been good to everyone.
Only some people are dour,
and when she gives them the come
hither with her eyes, they look down
or turn away and lift an eyebrow.
But me, I give her the wink
and away we go.

WILLIAM ALLEN WHITE

OLD SUPERSTITIONS

The maid who on the first of May
Goes to the fields at break of day
And washes in dew from the hawthorn tree,
Will ever after handsome be.

Gemini-The Twins

May 21– June 20

Gemini is one
  Of the intellectual Signs,
And Geminians often
  Have brilliant minds.
They like solving problems
  And answering questions,
Though they tend to ignore
  Advice and suggestions.
They're loaded with talent
  To get the job done,
And when their work's finished,
  They know how to have fun!

Things to do on your birthday
under the Sign of Gemini:

Have a neighborhood coffee.
Go to the public library
and check out a book.
Ride a bicycle.

June

And what is so rare as a day in June?
　　Then, if ever, come perfect days;
Then Heaven tries earth if it be in tune,
　　And over it softly her warm ear lays;
Whether we look, or whether we listen,
We hear life murmur, or see it glisten....

JAMES RUSSELL LOWELL

Oh for boyhood's time of June,
Crowding years in one brief moon,...
I was rich in flowers and trees,
Hummingbirds and honeybees...
Laughed the brook for my delight
Through the day and through the night....

JOHN GREENLEAF WHITTIER

A DAY OF SUNSHINE

O gift of God! O perfect day:
Whereon shall no man work, but play;
Whereon it is enough for me,
Not to be doing, but to be!

MY HEART LEAPS UP

My heart leaps up when I behold
    A rainbow in the sky:
So was it when my life began;
So is it now I am a Man;
So be it when I shall grow old,
    Or let me die!

WILLIAM WORDSWORTH

Let us, then, be up and doing,
    With a heart for any fate;
Still achieving, still pursuing,
    Learn to labor and to wait.

HENRY W. LONGFELLOW

SOMETIMES

Across the fields of yesterday
   He sometimes comes to me,
A little lad just back from play—
   The lad I used to be.

And yet he smiles so wistfully
   Once he has crept within,
I wonder if he hopes to see
   The man I might have been.

THOMAS S. JONES, JR.

O my love is like a red, red rose,
   That's newly sprung in June.
O my love is like the melodie,
   That's sweetly play'd in tune.

ROBERT BURNS

Cancer-The Crab

June 21— July 22

Those born under Cancer
  May be sensitive and shy,
But they display persistence
  In everything they try.
Though basically domestic,
  They sometimes like to roam,
But they're never really happy
  Until they're snug at home.
They have a talent for creating
  Harmony around them,
And their warmth insures
  That friends and family
Always will surround them.

Things to do on your birthday under the Sign of Cancer:

Sail a toy boat in the park.
Create a new recipe.
Try your hand at painting a landscape.

32

July

Flower - *Larkspur*　　　Birthstone - *Ruby*

When the scarlet cardinal tells
　　Her dream to the dragonfly,
And the lazy breeze makes a nest in the trees
　　And murmurs a lullaby,
　　　　It is July.

When the tangled cobweb pulls
　　The cornflower's cap awry,
And the lilies tall lean over the wall
　　To bow to the butterfly,
　　　　It is July.

When the heat like a mist veil floats,
　　And poppies flame in the rye,
And the silver note in the streamlet's throat
　　Has softened almost to a sigh,
　　　　It is July.

When the hours are so still that time
　　Forgets them, and lets them lie
'Neath petals pink till the night stars wink
　　At the sunset in the sky,
　　　　It is July.

SUSAN HARTLEY SWETT

The republic is a dream.
Nothing happens unless first a dream.

CARL SANDBURG

The autumn with its fruits provides disorders
for us, and the winter's cold turns them into sharp
diseases, and the spring brings flowers to strew
our hearse, and the summer gives green turf and
brambles to bind upon our graves.

JEREMY TAYLOR

For all your days prepare
  And meet them ever alike:
When you are the anvil, bear—
  When you are the hammer, strike.

EDWIN MARKHAM

Half our life is spent in trying to find something
to do with the time we have rushed through life
trying to save.

WILL ROGERS

34

WHEN WE LAY OUR DOLLS AWAY

What is it, dear heart? "Too big for dolls?"
  Is that what the wise folks say?
You "must say good-bye to your childhood
      friends,
  For you're twelve years old today"?
The dear little lady with flaxen hair
  And the darling with black eyes bright,
And—dearest of all—the "raggedy doll"—
  Must be hidden away from sight?

Ah, dear little girl, I know, I know;
  For the very saddest day
Is the day that comes to us, one and all,
  When we lay our dolls away;
The beautiful doll of Innocence,
  And the sturdy doll called Truth,
And—saddest of all—the "raggedy doll"—
  The unquestioning faith of youth!

FLORENCE A. JONES

Leo-The Lion

July 23—August 22

Leonians are dynamic;
    They were born to lead!
People admire them
    And that's what they need.
They have their stormy times
    Every now and then,
But the very next minute
    They're sunny again.
They're ruled by the sun,
    And maybe that's why
They can reach any goal
    No matter how high.

*Things to do on your birthday
under the Sign of Leo:*

Compliment a total stranger.
Write a Letter to the Editor.
Buy (and wear) an orange shirt.

August

Flower - *Gladiolus*   Birthstone - *Peridot*

RAIN IN AUGUST

The cool gray curtain of the rain
shuts softly down, and closes in
behind its slanting silver-thin
tissues, a winter peace again;

no sound comes through except the brush
of light folds over velvet grass
where misty garments flutter, pass
with healing in their blessed hush.

FLORENCE B. JACOBS

Every man's life is a fairy tale written by
God's fingers.

HANS CHRISTIAN ANDERSEN

A SUMMER RAMBLE

The quiet August noon has come;
A slumberous silence fills the sky,
The fields are still, the woods are dumb,
In glassy sleep the water lies.

Away! I will not be, today,
The only slave of toil and care;
Away from desk and dust! away!
I'll be as idle as the air.

Beneath the open sky abroad,
Among the plants and breathing things,
The sinless, peaceful works of God,
I'll share the calm the season brings.

Come, thou, in whose soft eyes I see
The gentle meaning of thy heart,
One day amid the woods with me,
From men and all their cares apart.

WILLIAM CULLEN BRYANT

Virgo-The Virgin

August 23 — September 22

People born under Virgo
   Are loaded with charm,
And when they share a friendship,
   It's especially close and warm.
Order is their watchword,
   They carefully arrange things
And may not take it kindly
   If someone tries to change things.
Virgos are too modest
   To ever brag or boast,
But making people happy
   Is what pleases them the most.

Things to do on your birthday
under the Sign of Virgo:

Send flowers to a dear friend.
Take a puzzle to a shut-in.
Soak in a bubble bath
and listen to Chopin.

September

Flower - *Aster*   Birthstone - *Sapphire*

LABOR DAY

There you sit
On your lawn
My happy, sleepy neighbor—
Aren't you glad on Labor Day
There isn't any labor?

SHELLEY SILVERSTEIN

A Great Man is what he is,
because he was what he was.

AUTHOR UNKNOWN

I was young and foolish then;
now I am old and foolisher.

MARK TWAIN

SEPTEMBER

The goldenrod is yellow,
   The corn is turning brown,
The trees in apple orchards
   With fruit are bending down;

The gentian's bluest fringes
   Are curling in the sun;
In dusty pods the milkweed
   Its hidden silk has spun;

The sedges flaunt their harvest
   In every meadow nook,
And asters by the brookside
   Make asters in the brook.

From dewy lanes at morning
   The grapes' sweet odors rise;
At noon the roads all flutter
   With yellow butterflies—

By all these lovely tokens
   September's days are here,
With summer's best of weather
   And autumn's best of cheer.

HELEN HUNT JACKSON

GROWING OLD

A little more tired at close of day,
A little less anxious to have our way;
A little less ready to scold and blame,
A little more care of a brother's name;

A little more love for the friends of youth,
A little less zeal for established truth;
A little more charity in our views,
A little less thirst for the daily news;

A little more leisure to sit and dream,
A little more real the things unseen;

A little more laughter, a few more tears,
And we shall have told our increasing years;
The book is closed, and the prayers are said,
And we are a part of the countless dead.
Thrice happy, if then some soul can say,
"I live because he has passed my way."

R. J. WELLS

Libra-The Scales

September 23 — October 22

Librans are delightful folks
  With good looks and friendly ways;
They view life as a picnic,
  And good fortune fills their days.
They're generous, but now and then
  When there's something to be done,
Carefree Librans may decide
  To cut out and have some fun.
They have a set of high ideals
  To which they're always true,
And they're wonderfully successful
  At inspiring others, too.

Things to do on your birthday
under the Sign of Libra:

Dig out your high school yearbook
and have a good laugh.
Dig out your old love letters
and have a good cry.
Drink champagne.

October

Flower - *Calendula*   Birthstone - *Opal*

OCTOBER

October came down from the hills
   last night
And painted each housetop a cool,
   frosty white.
With autumn's gay magic
   and silver-tipped wand,
Draped a gray, misty veil over brooklet
   and pond.

Placed a pale, mellow haze
   on the silvery moon
And a flock of wild ducks
   on a placid lagoon;
She sampled the nuts
   from a gray squirrel's hoard
And tasted the sweets
   that the honeybee stored.

She climbed the tall elm
  on the hill's lofty crest
To hang a "for rent" sign
  on the oriole's nest.
She stopped at each thicket
  and vine-covered dell
To bid all the songbirds
  a tender farewell.

She shook from the bough
  of each hickory tree
A treasure to fill
  every schoolboy with glee.
In the orchard where apples
  hang high overhead,
She kissed every cheek
  till it blushed ruby-red.

She decked each tall maple
  in country and town
With a crimson corsage
  and a bright yellow gown.
Both poet and peasant
  are thrilled with delight;
October came down
  from the hills last night!

REGINALD HOLMES

AUTUMN

The morns are meeker than they were,
The nuts are getting brown;
The berry's cheek is plumper,
The rose is out of town.

The maple wears a gayer scarf,
The field a scarlet gown.
Lest I should be old-fashioned,
I'll put a trinket on.

EMILY DICKINSON

HALLOWEEN

O'er all there hung a shadow and a fear,
A sense of mystery the spirit daunted,
And said as plain as whisper in the ear,
    The place is Haunted!

THOMAS HOOD

Scorpio-The Scorpion

October 23 — November 22

Scorpios are famous
  For "doing their own thing,"
Regardless of the conflict
  Or problems it might bring.
They dominate the scene
  And do everything with zest,
Whether it's having a high old time
  Or facing a crucial test.
Self-contained and secretive,
  Scorpios seldom reveal
Their inner thoughts and feelings
  And their very high ideals.

*Things to do on your birthday
under the Sign of Scorpio:*

Go for a long walk in the park.
Write a love song.
Do something around the house
that you have been putting off
for a long time.

November

Flower - *Chrysanthemum*   Birthstone - *Topaz*

ORPHANED CHILD

November is a lonely waif
With wistful, wide-eyed ways,
Subdued by the flamboyance of
The bright October days,
And feeling very small before
December's sparkling glance.
Never mind, November, twirl
Your tattered skirts and dance,
Dance a bittersweet ballet
With the leaves that fly away!

DORIS CHALMA BROCK

Keep your eyes open to your mercies.
The man who forgets to be thankful
has fallen asleep in life.

ROBERT LOUIS STEVENSON

THE SNOW FALL

Quietness clings to the air.
Quietness gathers the bell
  To a great distance.
    Listen!
  This is the snow.
  This is the slow
    Chime
  The snow
    Makes.
  It encloses us.
Time in the snow is alone:
Time in the snow is at last,
    Is past.

ARCHIBALD MACLEISH

THE GREATER THING

Great it is to believe the dream
When we stand in youth by the starry
    stream;
But a greater thing
    is to fight life through
And say at the end, "The dream
    was true."

EDWIN MARKHAM

These then are my last words to you,
Be not afraid of life.
Believe that life is worth living
and your belief will help create the fact.

WILLIAM JAMES

THANKSGIVING

We thank Thee, Lord, for giving us
Thy gift of bread and meat.
We thank Thee, too—a little more—
That we are here to eat!

LEVERETT LYON

54

Sagittarius-The Archer

November 23 — December 21

Those born under Sagittarius
  Like to laugh and have fun.
You can count on them to be honest
  And fair with everyone.
When it comes to solving problems,
  A Sagittarian is a whiz,
For he knows how to face the facts
  And "tell it like it is."
They seldom, if ever, ask for help —
  But they're always glad to give it —
And life will always be their joy
  For they know just how to live it!

*Things to do on your birthday
under the Sign of Sagittarius:*

Call up a friend whom you have not seen
  for several months and go to lunch.
    Acquire a new hobby.
Write a poem about the beauty of nature.

December

Flower - *Narcissus* Birthstone - *Turquoise*

WINTER

Then comes the winter, like a hale old man
Wrapped in his cloak with frosty locks
    and beard.
Winter is the time for clear,
    cold starlight nights,
And driving snows, and frozen roads
    and rivers,
For crowding round the blazing
    Christmas fire,
For telling tales that make the blood
    run cold,
For sipping elder-wine
    and cracking filberts,
For friendships, chilblains, fun,
    roast beef, mince pies,
And shivering fits on jumping into bed:
And thus the year goes round,
    and round, and round.

JAMES HURNARD

57

A DECEMBER DAY

Dawn turned on her purple pillow,
    And late, late, came the winter day;
Snow was curved to the boughs of the willow,
    The sunless world was white and grey.
At noon we heard a blue jay scolding,
    At five the last cold light was lost
From blackened windows faintly holding
    The feathery filigree of frost.

SARA TEASDALE

How beautiful the lights of Chanukah...
Kindled forever in the heart of Israel,
Lights of Torah,
    Justice and Mercy,
        Lights of Courage,
            Patience and Love,
Lights to praise the Lord
And fill every home with His blessings.

DAVID BEN LEVI

58

It is good to be children sometimes,
and never better than Christmas time
when its mighty founder was a child Himself.

CHARLES DICKENS

I WISH THEE

What shall I wish thee
   for the coming year?
Twelve months of dreamlike ease?
   no care? no pain?
Bright spring, calm summer,
   autumn without rain
Of bitter tears? Wouldst have it thus,
   my friend?
What lessons, then, were learnt
   at the year's end?

What shall I wish thee then?
   God knoweth well
If I could have my way no shade of woe
Should ever dim thy sunshine;
   but I know
Strong courage is not learnt
   in happy sleep,

Nor patience sweet by eyes
   that never weep.

Ah, would my wishes were
   of more avail
To keep from thee the many jars
   of life!
Still let me wish thee courage
   for the strife,
The happiness that comes from work
   well done—
And, afterwards, the peace
   of victory won!

Set in Walbaum, a light, open typeface
designed by Justus Erich Walbaum (1768-1839),
who was a typefounder at Weimar. Printed on
Hallmark Eggshell Book paper.
Designed by Claudia Becker.